THE REBEL WITHIN

THE REBEL WITHIN

A Guide to Challenging
Your Inner Critic and
Discovering Your Authentic Self

Iñaki Escudero

*To my father and my mother for allowing me to have
an authentic voice.*

To my 5 children for the sound of your voice.

To my brothers, your childhood voices echo through my life.

To my friends, for welcoming the sound of my voice.

And especially to my wife Hazel, for celebrating my voice.

BEFORE WE START

Allow me to address something potentially awkward: We're probing into the complexity of your brain and how it works, particularly your inner voice and sub-conscious. In essence, we'll be using your brain to absorb and process information about itself, and yes, it might feel a bit awkward, perhaps even uncomfortable at times.

Your inner voice may suggest that you're already acquainted with the stories I've shared here or, perhaps, dismiss the advice provided in each chapter as outdated and irrelevant to your current situation.

Let me assure your inner voice that our intent is purely beneficial. You are, in fact, the protagonist of this narrative. The entire book revolves around you. So, take a moment to relax; you might find the journey quite enjoyable.

TABLE OF CONTENTS

OH NO!
ANOTHER SELF-HELP BOOK

Hello reader, thank you for picking up this book. I know the title reads like a self-help book, the book looks like a self-help book, and the book was classified as a self-help title. I don't blame you for being confused. But you see, I had to get your inner voice's attention. And these types of books are the ones that your inner dialogue tends to pick when tempted to choose a book.

Recent research identified approximately 3,700 American book titles beginning with the words 'how to'. And as of 2021, the personal development market generated an estimated $41.81 billion in revenue worldwide, and such a large market means people love this stuff. Whatever stage of your life you want to fine-tune, chances are high that someone's already written a book about it.

The promise of improvement and transformation is very appealing. And self-help books offer such alluring stories of self-improvement and well-being.

The goal is clear: To enhance personal strengths and functioning through personal growth.

I read a lot of books. Not as many as some, but I read more than most. Many of those books are self-help books. And every time I finish one, I feel inspired to do better and I'm energized to try the advice offered by the author. It's a great feeling of possibility and optimism: I can do better, I can feel better, I can be better.

It's empowering.

But unfortunately, it doesn't last very long.

After a few successful days of keeping up with a new routine and well-intended commitments, I go back to old habits and behaviors.

Believe me, I've tried. Self-awareness, meditation, yoga, keto, vitamins, retreats, mindfulness, gratitude journals, growth mindset, deep breathing, cold showers. I've tried them all.

But the truth is that achieving real, tangible change is hard for us humans.

A few days ago, I started to wonder: Why is it so hard to change for the better?

The arguments are compelling, the research supports the benefits, and the benefits are positive and life-improving. So, why is it so challenging to implement these learnings? So hard to help myself become a better person and live a better, happier life?

Then yesterday, during my daily run, it hit me: It's our inner voice.

Yes, "the voice inside your head," your "internal dialogue," your "inner speech."

This inner voice can be helpful and encouraging: I'm good. I can do that! or I will get it right.

But it can also be critical, pessimistic, and negative: I'm not good at this, I'll fail, or I don't deserve this.

And we believe this voice because it is our own voice, but that's the real problem. This voice doesn't know what's best for you any better than a random stranger from the street would.

Why, you ask?

Because we are only human. And humans, in all our amazingness, are inherently imperfect.

First, our inner voice is influenced by cognitive biases that tend to favor information that confirms existing beliefs.

Second, our inner voice often resists change because it prioritizes familiarity and comfort. Third, experiences from the past, especially negative ones, may lead to self-limiting beliefs and decisions that prioritize avoiding perceived threats.

And finally, because many people operate on autopilot without deep self-awareness.

Our inner voice, in essence, doesn't have a big incentive for us to be successful in changing, even if it's clearly for the better.

It's with this spirit that I wrote this book: to awaken your **rebel within**, challenge your inner voice's instincts, and offer you a real chance at improvement.

You see, it's not a self-help book after all; it's a help-your-inner-voice book.

Chapter 1

I CAN'T RUN ANYMORE

I was 16 years old when my soccer career came to an end due to a broken Anterior Cross Ligament and two meniscus injuries, marking the conclusion of my time in the sport, and my dreams of becoming a professional soccer player.

This type of injury is among the worst a player could endure in any sport, especially in soccer, and particularly in 1981.

Back then, unless you were a professional player, you didn't receive the "respect" the injury deserved. I was told: if you are not making a living from your legs, "why would you go through the pains of fixing and recovering like a professional."

Yes, it may not be the brightest diagnosis in medicine's history, but it's the one I got.

I still had to have two surgeries done to get rid of bone chips inside my right knee, which had me in bed, in a cast, and in recovery for the good part of two years.

Seventeen years of "feeling sorry for myself" later, I took a look at myself in the mirror and didn't like what I saw. Overweight, out of shape, two-pack-per-day chain-smoker I had had enough.

I decided I had to do something drastic to prove to myself I was still an athlete.

In May 1999, I signed up to run the New York Marathon that November.

When I began training, I couldn't finish a mile. But I was committed, and I followed every step in the training program. When my knee got swollen, I iced it, and when it hurt, I braced it. When I got tired, I rested.

I finished the marathon in 3 hours and 58 minutes. Even though I was ecstatic about finishing the race, my knee bothered me for the next 4 months.

I went to see a doctor who recommended another intervention to remove more bone chips still floating around my knee.

I continued to run one marathon per year. Chicago, Marine Corps, Twin Cities, Dallas. More swollen knee, more ice, and more recovery.

At this point, I should have stopped running, but I didn't. And in 2008 my body made a decision my mind couldn't. I developed a bad IT band condition.

Science break: The iliotibial (IT) band is a thick band of connective tissue that runs along the outside of the thigh, from the hip to the knee. IT band syndrome is a condition where the IT band becomes tight or inflamed, causing (a lot of) pain on the outer side of the knee.

It kept me from running for 5 years.

Full disclaimer: I also had 5 children, a busy job, and very little free time. Let's not blame it all on the injury. If this book is about coming clean with yourself, let's do it.

All right, truth be told, my inner voice insisted that my running years were over.

In 2013 I got the running bug again and ran the New York City Marathon, again.

I followed all the precautions and routines I had developed during my earlier marathon running years, the knee brace, the ice, the resting, the stretching, the caution.

At this point, it's worth sharing that I felt like I was a runner again. I was running three times per week, doing about 250 miles per year.

And then a funny thing happened; I broke what was left of my meniscus again, building a toy kitchen for my girls at Christmas. It was really funny. The doctor who did the surgery told me afterward (again) that running of any kind was probably not the best idea.

In 2020, I decided to start going to the gym. One of those New Year resolutions, you know?

Well, part of the experience requires running on a treadmill for 1-3 miles. Because I was committed to making the gym membership count, I was going to the gym every day.

As you can imagine, my main concern was, will my knee be able to run every day? I had never done it before; in 20 years since my first marathon, I had never run two days in a row, let alone 5, or 10, or 20.

What would you know, my knee didn't get swollen, I didn't feel any pain, and I didn't have to ice it.

67 days in a row running and I was feeling better than ever, until Covid forced all public venues to shut down!

Solution, don't stop, go out for a run, 1 mile every day, see how it feels.

No pain!

What if we go up to 3 miles per day?

No pain.

After 2 months, I was running 6 miles per day, with no pain at all. I was running faster, and longer than ever before.

I wanted to understand what had changed, and I realized that the only significant change had happened inside of me. I had stopped telling myself all the things I couldn't do and instead, I told myself all the things I could do.

I stopped dwelling on perceived limitations and focused on my capabilities as a runner.

I silenced the inner voice that insisted on my incapacity to run, replacing it with a new narrative proclaiming that I was indeed a runner.

Today I run injury-free, I run every day, and I run faster, stronger, and further than ever.

This change in the inner dialogue has propelled me to complete 13 marathons since 2020, culminating in 1,400 total miles run in 2023.

I have gone from trusting and listening to my cautious inner voice to rebelling against it with my actions.

This battle is an ongoing struggle inside my brain. The coutious Iñaki and the rebel Iñaki.

I think this story will help bring to life what's going on inside our heads.

The Tale of Two Wolves:

An old Cherokee is teaching his grandson about life. "A fight is going on inside me," he said to the boy.

"It is a terrible fight, and it is between two wolves. One is evil - he is anger, envy, sorrow, regret, greed, arrogance, self-pity, guilt, resentment, inferiority, lies, false pride, superiority, and ego."

He continued, "The other is good - he is joy, peace, love, hope, serenity, humility, kindness, benevolence, empathy, generosity, truth, compassion, and faith. The same fight is going on inside you - and inside every other person, too."

The grandson thought about it for a minute and then asked his grandfather, "Which wolf will win?"

The old Cherokee simply replied, "The one you feed."

Chapter 2

TALK A GOOD GAME

Dr. Jim Loehr is an acclaimed performance psychologist, author, and co-founder of the Human Performance Institute. He is known for his expertise in motivation, mental toughness training, and developing the mental game required for peak performance.

He has worked extensively with world-class athletes over his career and is credited with helping many achieve new levels of sustained success in their sports.

One of the athletes he worked with was Dan Jansen, an American speed skater.

At both the 1988 and 1992 Olympics, Dan was the favorite to win the 500- & 1,000-meter races.

He didn't medal at either and the media tagged him as a "choker."

Dan's agent called Dr. Jim Loehr, and said,

"Would you consider working with Dan Jansen?"

So Jim said, "I know about Dan. I know about his story. I'd love to meet with him."

When they met for the first time Dr. Jim Loehr had learned about Dan's backstory: Hours before the 500-meter race at the '88 Olympics, Jansen received a phone call and learned that his 27-year-old sister died of leukemia.

This is how Jim tells the story: Dan was going to not skate. Then his father said, "What do you think Jane would want you to do?" He thought about it, and he said, "I think she would want me to skate." So he puts his skates on. He is in tears, and he tries to mobilize himself to just win this race and to get through it somehow. But he's completely off-center emotionally, and just a few feet into the start Dan Jansen falls. And Dan Jansen rarely falls. He just doesn't. So he felt a great sense of failure. Not only did he fail in the race, he failed her because he wanted to do something special for his sister.

Loehr started attending Jansen's training sessions, and after watching Dan skate over and over again, he became convinced that Dan's best shot at winning a gold medal was not in the 500, but in the 1,000.

"I asked Dan, "What would you like to finish your career with? What would be something that would be deeply satisfying?" And he said, "Well, I'd love to just have some kind of Olympic success. I mean, I've had none." He said, "This is my last Olympic event. I will not skate again. I'd like to have an Olympic victory of some kind. And I would like to break the 36-second barrier," which was thought at that time to be the barrier. It's like the four-minute mile for Roger Bannister. It's something that human beings will never be able to break.

I said, "Okay, I want you in your training logs for the remainder of your time, I want you to write 35:99. And I want you to start believing that that will be possible for Dan Jansen before the end of your career." And I said, "Now I'm going to ask you to do something else because I know you're going to resist this one. I want you to write on the top of your training log 'I love the 1,000,'" because Dan Jansen did not love the 1,000. He felt he was a fast-muscle twitch kind of a guy. He was a sprinter. He hated the endurance event. He always got tired. He just did it for training purposes. And I said, "Dan, I've watched you skate over and over and over again. And I can tell you, you have such genius. You could win an Olympic gold medal, even in the 1,000. I want you to begin to change your mindset, the story you have is around 1,000, and I believe it can change your life."

So for 2 years, at the top of his training log, Jansen wrote, "I love the 1,000."

Loehr adds, "We created a mindset, and the mindset we created was—instead of a gold medal or a world record or anything else—think about what a gift the sport of speed skating has been to you. Think about the joy it's brought you."

With that mindset, Jansen lined up for the 1,000-meter event at the 1994 Winter Olympics in Lillehammer.

With that mindset, he not only won his first Olympic gold medal, he set a new world record time in the 1,000.

In his work with hundreds of world-class performers, Dr. Loehr spent many years listening to the stories people tell themselves. "I spent so many years listening to the voices, trying to get inside the heads of players. We had them wear microphones and they were to articulate everything that they said to themselves during a competitive event. And whether it be in golf or tennis or whatever. And as I began to realize what really mattered, in a really significant way was the tone and the content, as you said of the voice no one hears. I came to understand that the ultimate coach for all of us in life is that private voice. And that private voice can be brutal, can actually be a detriment to being the best you can be."

"And I began to realize that what really matters, in a really significant way, is the tone and the content of the voice in your head," he said.

That voice, we don't even know where for sure it comes from, but we know it begins to form as early as five years of age. And it comes principally, from the authority figures in your life, the people who had the most influence in your life at that time. We take on their voices, however functional or dysfunctional, because we, in a sense, want to be like them. We want to grow up and be strong or whatever it is, independent like they were. And so we get all these voices in our head, and some of them are, if you had a rough father or if you had a mother who was particularly harsh or doting, or didn't want you to be involved in anything that you might get hurt. All those voices, it's not like they are not being somehow laid down in some way, particularly when the themes are consistent.

The power broker in your life is the voice that no one ever hears. How well you revisit the tone and content of that voice in your head is what determines the quality of your life. It is the master storyteller, and the stories we tell ourselves are our reality.

Dr. Jim Loehr finally concludes: "So I'm always encouraging athletes to develop their voice. Develop that private voice and make sure that whatever that voice is articulating to them, the advice, the languaging, and the tone, is something that that's how they would coach someone that they cared about because it's the best that you have to give. And that sometimes takes years to develop, but it's awareness. And it is a very tough thing."

Chapter 3

INNER VOICE, WE NEED TO TALK

On average, people have about 12,000 thoughts per day. And research by cognitive scientists like Eric Kandel indicates that about 30% of daily thoughts tend to be repeated from the previous day.

The exact number of thoughts and the degree of repetition varies greatly between individuals, and are hard to demonstrate accurately, but the point remains, a lot is going on inside our heads at any given minute of the day. Even subconsciously, while we are sleeping.

This constant stream of thoughts is also known as our inner voice.

Now, what is exactly our inner voice?

Our inner voice is your own personal narrator offering opinions, judgments, observations, reminders, and a running commentary on things.

The inner voice gives us a constant sense of internal self-referencing. It's shaped by our past experiences, present perceptions, assumptions, desires, and fears.

In essence; We are what we say to ourselves all day long.

From a scientific perspective, the inner voice is believed to be a product of complex neural activity in the brain. It involves the interplay of various brain regions responsible for language, memory, thought processing, and self-awareness. While there are some common attributes in how people experience their inner voices, the truth is that we all have unique inner voices.

When we are born, we start to develop our inner voice as we interact with our environment and try to make sense of it:

- Our senses are constantly receiving information from the environment, forming the raw material for our stories and inner dialogues.

- Our emotions and biases play a significant role in shaping our stories and inner voices. We tend to focus on information that confirms our existing beliefs and biases, often coloring our narratives with emotions, making them more vivid and impactful.

- Our social interactions also influence how we construct stories and inner voices. We learn from others, share our experiences, and adapt our narratives to fit within the social context.

- We rely on our memories to recall past experiences and events, which we then combine with our imaginations to create new narratives.

It is important to note that the mind actively constructs our experiences and shapes our perception of the world by combining input from our senses, emotions, social interactions, and memories. So our stories and inner voices are not simply reflections of reality; **they are interpretations and creations of the mind.**

The brain constantly predicts future events based on its past experiences. When new information is received, the brain compares it to its predictions and updates its internal model of the world. This process shapes how we interpret events and construct narratives. This is called Predictive Coding.

Because we are super social animals, our brain neurons activate both when we perform an action and when we observe someone else performing the same action. This helps us understand the intentions and emotions of others and may also be involved in the creation of our own inner voices.

The theory of Embodied Cognition suggests that the entire body, including its sensory-motor system, plays a crucial role in shaping thoughts, emotions, and perceptions. Our inner voice lives in our brain but is created by our whole-body experience.

That's why it's so important to recognize the role our inner voice plays in influencing our perception of reality. The stories we tell ourselves can either propel us forward, motivating positive actions and resilience, or limit us by fostering self-doubt, fear, and negative behavioral patterns.

Jon Sincero, the author of "You Are a Badass: How to Stop Doubting Your Greatness and Start Living an Awesome Life," encourages us to silence our inner critic, overcome self-doubt, and take control of our thoughts and actions.

I guess the main challenge is how.

How can we be both the inner voice and the voice, the observer and the observed, the brain and the mind?

In the upcoming chapters, we will explore this paradox in-depth.

We'll do it by dissecting the messages in some of the best-selling books in the self-help category and we'll explore how our inner voice is boycotting each of them.

I'll end each chapter indicating how to challenge and overcome your inner voice's excuses and offer you a real chance at personal improvement.

Chapter 4

YOUR INNER VOICE IS ANCIENT

I know we would like to think that we are the smartest group of humans ever to roam the face of the earth, but we actually come from a long line of curious, smart, and capable individuals who suspected long before we did that there was something going on inside our head.

Traditional Chinese philosophy, including Confucianism and Taoism, emphasizes the importance of inner harmony, and the inner voice is often associated with aligning one's actions with broader cosmic principles.

The Egyptians believed in a concept called "Ba," a soul component residing in the heart and acting as the voice of conscience.

The Greeks conceptualized the inner voice as "daimon," a personal spirit or guide influencing thoughts and actions.

In Buddhism, they have the concept of "Manas," where the mind acts as the seat of thoughts and desires, requiring training to achieve inner peace.

In many Indigenous Cultures, the inner voice is viewed as connected to the natural world, receiving guidance from spirits and ancestral wisdom.

More recently, Maslow's concept of self-actualization highlighted the importance of listening to the inner voice to achieve one's full potential.

Contemporary spiritual and New Age movements like Meditation and Mindfulness encourage cultivating awareness of the inner voice, allowing for self-observation and non-judgmental acceptance.

Interpretations of the inner voice have evolved across cultures and historical periods, reflecting the broader philosophical, religious, and societal contexts in which they emerge.

But one constant across most of these interpretations is the dual role the inner voice plays: On one side, if we can borrow from Christian symbolism, we can find the white Angel standing on one of your shoulders, and on the other, a red angel — both inner voices present at the same time, both competing for your attention, both telling you compelling stories about reality.

Which one do we choose?

Chapter 5

A ROLLERCOASTER JOURNEY TO SELF-DISCOVERY

The Alchemist" by Paulo Coelho follows a young Andalusian shepherd named Santiago on a quest to fulfill his Personal Legend. Guided by a recurring dream and a mysterious king named Melchizedek, Santiago leaves his comfortable but unfulfilling life to pursue his treasure in the Egyptian pyramids.

Along his journey, Santiago encounters various characters who teach him valuable lessons about life, love, and the pursuit of dreams. He learns to overcome challenges, face his fears, and trust his intuition. He discovers the power of the present moment, the importance of listening to his heart, and the interconnectedness of all things.

The book has inspired thousands of people to pursue their own Personal Legend; the unique path or purpose that each person is meant to follow in their life.

I love the idea of having a higher meaning and being destined to live my own adventure.

Chances are, the second I'm ready to book that trip to my next great adventure, my inner voice might suggest that perhaps this is a big waste of time and money. Perhaps my purpose is to live a safe, comfortable, and long life. Perhaps my intuition is wrong. Perhaps dreams are for dreamers, and I am a realist.

Humans have evolved to build safe, reliable environments that we can trust to guarantee our safety. Of course, our inner voice is going to scream bloody Mary when contemplating the option of pursuing our dreams, taking risks, and embracing failures.

But here is the thing: when we seek intuitive guidance as the book proposes, we can't let our inner voice distract us with rational arguments.

Intuition is not a thought; it's a feeling. It's a sense of understanding without the need for conscious analysis. Intuition is our inner voice's kryptonite.

Our inner voice hates the unknown, and it mostly lives in the past and the future. Since "The Alchemist" inspires us to let our intuition guide us in the future pursuit of our Personal Legend, this creates tension between being inspired by the book's recommendations and our inner voice's need for safety.

One of the main lessons of the book is captured in this quote: "The secret of life, though, is to fall seven times and to get up eight times."

The inner voice's reaction? Maybe the secret of life is to avoid falling at all.

The Rebel within says you are not your thoughts. Mentally step back from your thoughts. Imagine viewing them from a neutral perspective rather than being fully immersed in them. Because the only way to discover who we truly are is when we embrace both our triumphs and our hardships.

Chapter 6

CHALLENGING
YOUR INNER VOICE

Change is often the hardest thing for people to do because it requires stepping out of one's comfort zone, embracing the unknown, and challenging familiar habits and routines.

As the Russian author Tolstoy once said: "Everyone thinks of changing the world, but no one thinks of changing himself."

The best-selling book "Atomic Habits" by James Clear offers a method for us to manage change successfully. Clear argues that lasting change doesn't require dramatic shifts but rather focuses on small, incremental improvements that compound over time.

If we could summarize the book in one line, it would say something like this: Habits are the compound interest of self-improvement.

I love this book and the principles it promotes. It's inspiring and practical. If any method is going to successfully negotiate with our inner voice, it is a method that lowers the stakes and requires a small investment.

The thing is, our inner voice doesn't negotiate with logic and reason.

I've seen it happening everywhere through my job as a change management facilitator. Smart executives, Ph. D.s and master's holders, engineers, and creatives alike understand why change is happening, why they need to adjust to a new reality, and they understand the process ahead. But when it comes down to it, change is a threat to the world as we know it, and our inner voice knows it.

Inner Voice: Other people need to change, not us. I can't change because... and because...

Change needs a system that helps the transition from one world to the other, from bad habits to building good, healthy habits, as James Clear explains.

But you see, the new system needs to coexist, at least for a while, with the old system, and that makes change even more challenging. Imagine running iOS and Windows on the same computer at the same time. Talking about an identity crisis!

But the biggest challenge the implementation of new habits faces is the short-term vs long-term feature of our brain. Our brain may prioritize instant gratification over delayed, but potentially greater, rewards. It's called "present bias" and gives our inner voice the fuel it needs to boycott our best intentions for the future betterment of our lesser nature.

The Rebel Within wants you to challenge your inner voice at the core: your value system, by aligning the new habits with what matters most to you. Also, take it one day at a time, focusing on the journey of learning and growth, and celebrate the small wins. Your inner voice will be sensitive to long-term plans that require drastic transformations, but when you break down large goals into tiny, achievable steps, you might lower your inner voice's fear of failure and uncertainty.

Chapter 7

THE TRUTHS YOUR INNER VOICE WANTS TO HIDE

"The Four Agreements" by Don Miguel Ruiz transcends the self-help category to become a life-changing philosophy. The book serves as a powerful guide to personal freedom and happiness, drawing wisdom from the Toltec people. Its core message revolves around cultivating personal freedom by challenging self-limiting beliefs.

The actual four agreements are: Be impeccable with your word, Don't take anything personally, Don't make assumptions, and Always do your best. By embracing these agreements and taking responsibility for our words, thoughts, and actions, the book suggests that we can unlock the doors to a life filled with freedom, love, and joy. (Note: There isn't a formal signing form.)

I have come to believe that we truly are what we practice. However, the challenge lies in years of practicing doubt, self-criticism, or internal gossiping, undermining the suggestions made by the book.

And don't get me started on our inner voice taking things personally or making assumptions. I think I could give a TED talk about these two subjects.

If your inner voice is overly critical (and whose isn't, right?), it might set unrealistic standards, fostering self-blame if one falls short of perceived expectations.

During the inner dialogue with ourselves, we often give too much credit to the arguments used by the inner voice because they come from inside our minds. (Paradox moment.) But this voice is not you; it's not even we. The brain, as a highly efficient organ, has evolved to preserve energy and ensure the body's survival. It does so by developing mental models, cognitive shortcuts, and strategies that help in decision-making and daily functioning.

It's important to understand the concept of Homeostasis: when the brain seeks to maintain a state of physiological and psychological equilibrium. This can result in resistance to change, as the brain may interpret change as a potential threat to the stability it has established.

So here it is, the turret is our inner voice that has an agenda, and that's why it may present arguments rooted in familiarity, comfort, and the avoidance of perceived risks associated with change.

The Rebel Within turns aspirational behaviors into daily practices, forcing the inner voice to accept that this is not a bug in the system but indeed a feature. Embracing intentional, positive actions as routine functions rewires the cognitive patterns, affirming that change is not a threat but an inherent capability waiting to be harnessed.

Chapter 8

EMBRACING THE MESS

Few books will speak so directly, so honestly, and so harshly about our human nature than "The Subtle Art of Not Giving a F*ck" by Mark Manson.

In the process of discovering that accepting our limitations and embracing negative emotions can lead to a more fulfilling life, you will laugh at Mark's writing and fresh perspective. His book doesn't read like a self-help book, but it is indeed engaging and thought-provoking. I think you'll learn a lot from it.

The main takeaway, perhaps, is that by embracing our limitations and focusing on what truly matters, we can cultivate greater self-acceptance, resilience, and ultimately, a more fulfilling life.

I also enjoyed this quote a lot because it helped me understand my purpose with more clarity: "Who you are is defined by what you're willing to struggle for."

I personally found a lot of clarity in his concept of how meaning is created. He says: There is no inherent meaning in life; we create it through our values, relationships, and contributions.

And here is when it gets messy for me because meaning and purpose might sound like similar concepts, but they are not.

It took some thinking to understand the difference:

Meaning refers to the inherent significance or value of something.

While purpose is the sense of aim or determination to achieve a particular outcome.

I've read enough books to learn that alignment between our actions, our purpose, and our values is the ultimate nirvana. But why is it so hard to achieve that alignment?

Of course, I blame my inner voice.

Our inner voice is a storyteller, one of the best. And even when we have clearly defined our goals and aspirations, the inner voice can either motivate or demotivate us in the pursuit of them. Your inner voice keeps the score. And it remembers all the culture, social norms, and family belief systems that shaped it. This means that it reinforces or challenges the alignment between our actions and what we perceive as meaningful based on our core beliefs.

It's messy, I told you.

Even if I want to follow the book's recommendation of being selective about what to give a f*ck about, about taking responsibility for my actions, or about embracing negative emotions and failures; my inner voice will push back with my own mental models and core beliefs!

Messy, messy, messy.

The Rebel Within knows that your inner voice has created automated responses to specific situations, like exciting new changing routines, or positive encouragement.

Your rebellious self reframes those automatic responses by examining the evidence and evaluating if they reflect objective reality. This is known as cognitive restructuring or cognitive reappraisal, and its goal is to shift perspectives, challenge distorted thinking, and promote more balanced and constructive thinking.

Chapter 9

THE COURAGEOUS CONVERSATION

"Who Moved My Cheese?" by Spencer Johnson is a simple parable about change and adapting to new circumstances. It follows the story of four characters, two mice, and two little people, who live in a maze searching for cheese, a metaphor for what we desire in life, such as success, security, or happiness.

• Sniff and Scurry, the mice: These adaptable creatures constantly explore the maze, anticipating changes and adjusting their route accordingly.

• Haw and Hem, the little people: Initially complacent and resistant to change, they cling to their familiar cheese source until it disappears, forcing them to confront their fears and adapt.

"Who Moved My Cheese?" offers a simple yet powerful message about the importance of adaptability and resilience in the face of change. It encourages readers to embrace the unknown, learn from challenges, and continually seek new opportunities for growth and fulfillment.

The book has sold over 50 million copies worldwide and has been translated into over 47 languages. It was even selected in the "100 Most Influential Business Books of All Time" by Time Magazine.

One of the main lessons from the story encourages people to ask themselves this question: What would we do if we weren't afraid?

When I read the book, I was inspired by this message and started to ask questions in workshops with leaders from some of the most successful global companies. After discussing the new business environment and the new skills leaders needed to develop to thrive under change, the groups were ready to openly discuss this question.

And you wouldn't believe it, but in most cases, the first to speak would be the one with the objection, the person whose inner voice had stated: "We are not afraid! It's them who need to change, not me. It's all their fault."

As much as change is the only constant in life and affects all of us equally, some people think that it's not their problem, not their responsibility, not their problem to solve. Until it's too late.

The Rebel Within recognizes the ego's voice when it becomes critical, arrogant, or self-centered. Observe your inner voice's thoughts and emotions without

judgment. And here comes the courageous part: Forgive your inner voice's ego-driven mistakes, be kind to yourself, and appreciate the times your inner voice provides support and confidence. Remember, the best version of any type of work, even yourself, requires the courage to do the daily work.

Chapter 10

WISDOM AND COMPASSION

"The Gifts of Imperfection" by Brené Brown explores the importance of embracing our imperfections and vulnerabilities to live a wholehearted life.

Brown challenges societal expectations of perfectionism and encourages readers to cultivate self-compassion, courage, and authenticity. This involves accepting ourselves for who we are, allowing ourselves to be seen and heard, and taking risks to pursue our dreams.

Her main point is that vulnerability means strength, not weakness.

I'm a big fan of Brené Brown. I listen to her podcast, Courage to Lead. I have read many of her books, and I love her storytelling style. I think she is the first author I remember reading who spoke openly about vulnerability as a step to becoming authentic. (Authenticity is the foundation of a happy and fulfilling life.)

I grew up watching sports on TV with my family, and I've always used sports metaphors to make sense of the ups and downs of life. So it makes sense that I often think about my inner voice as a tough but kind sports coach. You know the type; they might get mad when you don't hustle enough or when you don't think about your team, but in their heart, they want to develop the character we need to be successful in the sport and in life.

That's my inner voice, well that's how I imagine my gentler inner voice. As a kind but tough coach, she wants the best for me, and she wants me to grow to be as good as I can be.

She expects me to be as good as other people around me are, and she is really disappointed when I don't perform at my best when it matters.

You see? My coach, who knows me well and has the best for me in mind, doesn't agree with Brené. Respects her, but disagrees with her.

The Rebel Within prefers an inner voice that acts as a facilitator rather than a coach. At the end, the best mentors are truly facilitators at heart. Your inner voice's wisdom comes down to facilitating planning, critical thinking, and cognitive flexibility. But more importantly, your inner voice's key job is to regulate emotions. In one word, be compassionate. She should help you calm down, manage stress, and maintain emotional stability, especially through difficult situations.

Chapter 11

THE HONEST MIRROR

The first book my father ever gave me with the intent of educating me was "How to Win Friends and Influence People" by Dale Carnegie. I was 9 years old.

My inner voice is wondering if there was a lost message my father tried to share with me that day.

I read the book with intent, since my father had suggested its importance. It had to be good.

I remember liking it. I also remember one lesson from the book. The sound people like the most is their own name.

I also realized, when doing the research for this book that I perhaps missed a more important lesson: The only way to get the best of an argument is to avoid it.

But more about that in a second.

This book is a classic, timeless self-help book that offers practical advice on interpersonal skills and effective communication. First published in 1936, the book has had a profound and lasting impact on society.

The book promotes a positive and empathetic approach to interpersonal relationships. The advice on dealing with people and building relationships is as applicable today as it was when the book was first published. Carnegie even emphasizes the importance of effective communication, teaching readers how to express themselves clearly, listen actively, and resolve conflicts constructively.

So, what problem could my inner voice have with such positive and encouraging advice?

Ah, good question.

Let's add another layer to the complex personality of our inner voice. Imagine an over-caffeinated, social-media-savvy commentator with a penchant for over-analyzing every situation, a hyperactive storyteller weaving narratives based on past experiences, and a cinematic director projecting vivid mental images onto the screen of your consciousness. Our inner voice is a dynamic blend of our deepest thoughts, the echoes of our past, and the live commentary on our present.

This stream of consciousness might value social activities one second and appeal to your introverted side the next. It might value the art of persuasion one day, and judge you as manipulative the next. It might encourage you to seek external validation and remind you that that self-worth should come from within the next.

If we are the average of the 5 people we spend the most time with, the Rebel Within becomes very intentional in surrounding itself with positive influences. The inner voice is a truth mirror, and we end up imitating the people and content we consume. Surround yourself with supportive individuals who uplift and encourage you. Also limiting exposure to negativity helps maintain a positive and nurturing narrative of yourself.

Chapter 12

LEARN TO SEE

"The Little Prince" by Antoine de Saint-Exupéry is a timeless tale about a young prince from a tiny asteroid who travels the universe, learning about life and humanity through his encounters with various characters.

This is what happens:

The Little Prince leaves his beloved rose behind and visits planets inhabited by eccentric adults, each representing a flaw or limitation of humankind: a king obsessed with power, a vain man seeking admiration, a drunkard, a businessman, a lamplighter, and a geographer. Each encounter offers him a glimpse into the absurdity and pitfalls of human behavior, highlighting themes like loneliness, greed, pride, and the pursuit of meaningless things. On Earth, he befriends a pilot stranded in the desert, learning about love, friendship, and the importance of human connection. He encounters a fox who teaches him the true meaning of friendship and the value of taming relationships.

I have to be honest; "The Little Prince" is not considered a self-help book. Yet, it has helped me so much.

That's why it makes the list of amazing books to guide you through life.

One of the iconic quotes from the book is: *"On ne voit bien qu'avec le cœur. L'essentiel est invisible pour les yeux"* ("One sees clearly only with the heart. What is essential is invisible to the eye"). The Little Prince learns that true understanding goes beyond appearances and is felt through the heart.

I see two interpretations of this: One, the heart, in this context, symbolizes a deeper knowledge that transcends rational thought. It suggests that true understanding comes not just from what we see on the surface but from a more profound sense of knowing that goes beyond appearances.

And two, the heart is often associated with the seat of emotions and the soul in many cultural and philosophical traditions. Learning to understand through the heart implies connecting with a deeper, more spiritual part of ourselves. It suggests that genuine understanding involves tapping into a wisdom that goes beyond the intellect and into the realm of the soul.

Now, back to our inner voice. The heart, in a metaphorical sense, can also be linked to our inner voice.

In which case, what's essential is invisible!!! What's more important than the inner voice that knows you, understands you, cares for you, and guides you with the quiet wisdom of your own truths, echoing the depth of your soul's connection to the world around you?

In summary: For us to see what truly matters; love and connection, we need to embrace our inner child (a sense of imagination, wonder, and open-minded curiosity) so we can overcome the assumptions and initial judgments of our inner voice.

The Rebel Within reminds us of what was once our natural disposition: Maintaining childlike wonder and imaginative insight helps us see and appreciate what truly matters in life.

Chapter 13

UNMASKING THE IMPOSTER

If the main purpose of our brain is to keep us alive, the main purpose of our consciousness is to make meaning of the world around us.

Many of you will think that ultimately our purpose is to be happy.

And that's where our last self-help book comes into play. "Stumbling on Happiness" is a book written by Daniel Gilbert, a professor of psychology at Harvard University. Published in 2006, the book explores the science of happiness and the ways in which humans perceive and pursue it. Gilbert is known for his work in the field of affective forecasting, which involves predicting one's emotional state in the future.

The main takeaway: Our brains are not wired to accurately predict what will make us happy in the long run.

Our inner voice, influenced by biases, expectations, and personal narratives, contributes to these imperfect predictions. Our inner voice may create narratives about what we believe will bring us happiness, which may not align with reality.

We focus on the wrong things, make inaccurate pre-dictions, and compare ourselves to others. In short, our inner voice can lead us astray in the pursuit of meaningful happiness.

That's the work of the inner voice.

But we know better.

We know that we adapt to our circumstances, finding a new baseline of happiness regardless of major life events, good or bad.

We know that experiences provide richer and longer-lasting happiness than material possessions.

We know that strong social connections are crucial for well-being and happiness.

We know that focusing on the good things in your life can increase your overall happiness.

We know that stepping outside your comfort zone can lead to personal growth and unexpected joy.

We know that we can use our imaginations to create mental simulations of future experiences, allowing us to anticipate and shape our future happiness.

We know what do to, and we just need to allow our-selves to do it.

In his famous poem "Song of Myself," Walt Whitman, in a way only poets can, captures the complex functioning of the human mind.

"Do I contradict myself?

Very well then I contradict myself,

(I am large, I contain multitudes.)"

We all contain a multitude of inner voices—the critical, the encouraging, the worried, the nurturing, the creative, or the logical.

And we embody all of them. We are emotional and rational, critical and compassionate, afraid and brave. We are brilliant and imperfect. We are children and adults. We are lost and found.

Only when we fully accept the role we play as the "architects of our happiness," can we then become our authentic selves.

The Rebel Within accepts the challenge of pursuing a better self while immersed in the mess of living our daily lives. Because the virtue of living is found in the recognition of the possibility of a better self.

Marcus Aurelius, the Roman Emperor, and Stoic philosopher, said: "Very little is needed to make a happy life; it is all within yourself, in your way of thinking."

Chapter 14

THE POWER BROKER

In 2008, I read 4 books throughout the entire year. I lamented to my wife Hazel that, while I loved books and reading, I hadn't invested enough time in doing something I enjoyed so much.

Two months later, on the day of my birthday, I found 37 books waiting for me on top of the kitchen table. Hazel had bought all the books that were in my Amazon cart, which I was using as a wish list of "books to read in the future."

I accepted the challenge my wife had set out for me: If you like reading, read!

I planned to read one book per week and see how far I could go with that. Of course, my inner voice made the expected arguments:

Where are you going to find the time?

What if you don't like the book?

And how about your dyslexia?

You'll never do it!

Don't you have better things to do with your time?

This book is not good.

Don't finish it, nobody will ever know.

Books are expensive.

Most of the books were fascinating. It was easy to lose track of time as week 1, week 2, and week 3 went by.

I'll be honest; some books were more challenging to get into a flow, and sometimes it was impossible to keep up with the work, husband, father, and reading demands. But I was on a mission. I had a rhythm, and I was going to finish 52 books by year's end.

On December 29th, 2009, I finished my 52nd book of the year. I had done it. It felt really good to prove to myself that I was capable of making a commitment and seeing it through to the end.

I had read 52 books, but there were so many more great books left to read. By now I had almost 2-years' worth of books on my wish list.

Ok, I told myself, the real challenge is doing it 2 years in a row.

And in 2010 I read 53 books. (just to prove to myself that I could actually do better the second time around))

Ok, how about going for one more year?

I finished 54 in 2011. 53 in 2012, 64 in 2013, 58 in 2014, 63 in 2015, And 52 per year between 2016 and 2022.

By 2023 my inner voice had already normalized the challenge. And I just had to follow the routine of selecting a book and reading the book. After 14 years of reading a book per week, reading had become an easy daily habit.

So I decided to change the story I was telling myself. Instead of reading to prove to myself that I could do it, (even after 14 years), I was going to read because I liked reading books. (Remember my original complaint in 2009 was that I enjoyed reading but wasn't doing enough of it.)

So starting in 2023, freed from the restraining dare I had made to myself in 2009, I was going to read because I enjoy reading. No more inner voice reminding me of the challenge to keep me on pace. This time I would do it for my benefit and enjoyment.

In 2023 I read 70 books. (Goodreads became my reading network of preference and the site does a good job of keeping track of the titles I finished)

I was surprised to see that the year that I enjoyed reading the most was the year I didn't push myself to read. The first year in 14 I didn't try to stay with a schedule and the first year I didn't try to prove to myself that I could still read a book per week.

It turns out that the year I focused on doing something for the joy of it, is the year I silenced my critical inner voice.

I allowed myself to read and live one book at a time.

That's the main lesson I learned in 2023, and the moral of this book's story:

The rebel within rewrites the story because stories become destiny.

Chapter 15

FOR THE RECORD

Something interesting happened during the 2023 edition of the Golden Globes.

No, it has nothing to do with Taylor Swift.

Ali Wong and Steve Yeun made history by winning the Best Female and Best Male awards from their performances on the show Beef.

But I want to focus on what happened next.

Yeun walks to the stage, receives his award, and while contemplating this incredible moment for him and his career, he says, "So weird, the story I usually tell of myself to myself is one of isolation and separateness..."

Steve Yeun, right at the moment when he was recognized as one of the best actors of the year, speaks of the story his inner voice had built about his career as an actor; "a story of isolation and separateness."

Steve's award-winning performance in Netflix's show "Beef" wasn't an accident. He had previously played a beloved character in "The Walking Dead", had been nominated for an Oscar for his performance in the movie "Minari." And Time magazine named him one of the 100 most influential people in the world in 2021.

And yet, at the moment when most people are driven to thank the people who helped them go through the ups and downs of an acting career, Steve thought of his inner voice and the story he had heard countless times inside his head.

I think in many ways, we all can relate to Steve. "*I told you I would make it. I told you I would be successful, I told you to believe in me*" directed to nobody but yourself, your inner voice.

Maybe I have triggered in you a healthy curiosity to want to know more about this inner voice of ours. How does our mind build its inner voice? Where does it live? And what does modern science have to say about it.

We reviewed in Chapter 4 the early theories our ancestors developed to understand what this inner dialogue was and what role it played in our lives. But I think that it would be beneficial to quickly review what science has to say today about our inner voice.

It's interesting to note that during my research on the latest scientific theories about the inner voice, I discovered that the concept of the "inner voice" is often approached from various psychological and philo-sophical perspectives, and there isn't a single, widely accepted theory that universally explains it.

This is what we know: The inner voice is a complex cognitive process that plays an important role in exec-utive function, social cognition, memory, and our sense of self.

Psychologist Lev Vygotsky discovered in the 1930s that around the age of 2 or 3, children begin to vocal-ize their thoughts during play, and Vygotsky proposed that this externalized chatter transforms into internal-ized inner speech by the age of 5. Brain imaging stud-ies support this concept, revealing that the develop-ment of inner speech aligns with the maturation of neural connections between areas of the brain responsible for speech production and comprehen-sion, occurring around the same time in early child-hood.

According to Vygotsky, the details of what the inner voice says, and its emotional weight, are influenced by what your caregivers say and how they say it.

Our brain stores every event we have ever experi-enced, every person, and every place we've encoun-tered. However, not all experiences carry the same weight or relevance. Certain individuals, such as our parents or caregivers, hold a more significant influ-ence than others. Similarly, imprints during our formative years leave a deeper mark than those in subsequent years.

Given the impossibility of our brain being aware of every memory, thought, feeling, and idea, our mind operates at different levels of cognitive awareness known as the conscious, subconscious, and unconscious minds.

The Conscious Mind.

This is the part of your mind that you are actively aware of at any given moment. It includes your current thoughts, feelings, sensations, and perceptions. Some aspects of the inner voice might be conscious, especially when we deliberately engage in self-talk or make decisions.

The Subconscious Mind.

The subconscious mind handles all the automatic processes that keep our body and mind functioning, like breathing, digestion, and basic motor skills. It also stores readily accessible memories and information. Psychodynamic theories, such as those proposed by Sigmund Freud, suggest that certain aspects of the inner voice may originate from the subconscious mind, influencing conscious thoughts and actions.

The Unconscious Mind.

This is the least accessible part of the mind, containing repressed memories, hidden desires, and deep-seated beliefs. We are generally unaware of the contents of the unconscious, though they can influence our thoughts, emotions, and behaviors in subtle ways. The inner voice might encompass elements from the unconscious, including automatic thoughts and ingrained beliefs.

The Conscious mind is your here-and-now awareness. The Subconscious is remembered data just below awareness, while the unconscious exerts an unseen influence on our psychological state.

All of them contribute to building the voice, the tone, and the stories that become your inner voice.

From a Neuroscientific perspective, scientists have identified the Default Mode Network (DMN), which is a brain network active during rest and self-referential thinking. Some theories propose that inner voice activity is linked to the DMN, shedding light on the brain's role in self-generated thoughts. Since the DMN is characterized by coherent low-frequency oscillations. One theory states that the inner voice emerges from the brain's resting state activity.

As interesting as these theories are, the truth is, that the inner voice is different for all of us. Since it's built from our unique life experiences, it's influenced by our culture, our language, our mentors, our critics, our hobbies, and our traumas.

In short, the inner voice remains one of the biggest scientific mysteries of our time.

CONCLUSION

This, dear reader, is the end of the book, and the start of your journey.

I could give you more examples, explore other amazing self-help books, or share more personal experiences with you, but I believe you have grasped my point by now, so it's time to let your Rebel Within do the work.

Enjoy the transformative realization that life is change itself. Because when things change, there is a possibility of change making us better.

This book asks you the question: What if you could be intentional in creating that better, and true version of yourself?

Already within you, there is a force more powerful than any other material or substance in the universe: Your will.

The Rebel Within is your will.

Your will to use the power of self-control and discipline to refuse to be controlled by your inner voice.

Your will to develop the inner strength to create the version of yourself that you want to become.

The Rebel Within pushes us to build ourselves into anything we can imagine.

You are not your environment,

You are not your childhood,

You are not your past,

You are not your inner voice.

Robin Sharma said "When you control your thoughts, you control your mind. And when you control your mind you control your life."

Buddha suggested that "The mind is everything. What you think, you become."

More recently, Vincent Van Gogh instructs us: "If you hear a voice within you say 'you cannot paint,' then by all means paint, and that voice will be silenced."

Ultimately, the Rebel Within lives by this mantra: "The quieter you become, the more you can hear." - Rumi

This is what I have learned that I can share with you as my truth: there is within us an unlimited source of power, an authentic voice that urges us to become the best version of ourselves.

When we let that voice guide us, we are capable of achieving anything.

ANYTHING!

Take, for instance, reading 72 books in a year even after being diagnosed with dyslexia, or running your fastest marathon at 58 years old, and with an injured knee.

This is the Rebel Within.

Thank you for reading.

Iñaki Escudero

Printed by Amazon Italia Logistica S.r.l.
Torrazza Piemonte (TO), Italy

58822665R00040